PRIUS

Michael Bradley

mc Marshall Cavendish
Benchmark
New York

Marshall Cavendish Benchmark
99 White Plains Road
Tarrytown, NY 10591
www.marshallcavendish.us

All websites were available and accurate when this book was sent to press.

Library of Congress Cataloging-in-Publication Data

Bradley, Michael, 1962—
Prius / by Michael Bradley.
p. cm. — (Cars)
Includes bibliographical references and index.
ISBN 978-0-7614-4114-4
1. Prius automobile—Juvenile literature. 2. Hybrid electric cars—Juvenile literature. I. Title.
TL215.P78B73 2009
629.222'2—dc22
          2008049485

Editor: Megan Comerford
Publisher: Michelle Bisson
Art Director: Anahid Hamparian
Series Designer: Daniel Roode

Photo research by Connie Gardner

Cover photo by Ron Kimball/www.kimballstock.com

The photographs in this book are used by permission and through the courtesy of:
Ron Kimball/www.kimballstock.com: back cover, 1, 12, 16, 27, 28, 29; *Getty Images*: 18, 19, 20, 23;
Scott Halleran, 4; Alex Wong, 7; AFP, 24, 26; *AP Photo*: Paul Sakuma, 6; Amy Sancetta, 8;
Corbis: Car Culture, 10; Kimimasa Mayama/Reuters, 14; *Image Works*: Kathy McLaughlin, 25.

Printed in Malaysia
135642

CONTENTS

The Toyota Prius is certainly a special car. Buyers will wait for months to get their new Priuses! Displays such as this one at the 2004 Greater Los Angeles Auto Show made people even more excited about the car.

Steve Livingston was getting excited. By January 2004 he was eleventh on the waiting list for a Toyota Prius. Livingston, who lived in Newport Beach, California, was only a few months away from being the proud owner of a **hybrid** car. The wait was even longer at dealerships in Nevada and Arizona, so he felt lucky. Some people laughed at the idea of waiting several months for a new car. After all, the Prius wasn't a limited edition Ferrari or a custom-made **roadster**.

But the Prius is different than the usual automobile. Not only is it a car, but as a hybrid, it is also a statement. People who drive the Prius do so to make a difference. They lower their own gas costs and help the environment by driving a hybrid, which produces less poisonous gas than regular cars.

Prius owners don't have to fill up the gas tank as often as people who drive regular cars or SUVs. There was a big demand for Priuses when gas prices sky-rocketed in 2008.

When the Prius was first put on the market, **global warming** and **alternative fuel** sources were becoming hot topics and many people were going green by adopting environmentally friendly lifestyles—it was perfect timing. While some Americans were buying huge **sport-utility vehicles** (SUVs), many others were trying to **conserve** energy and cut down on pollution. For them, the chance to buy a car that did both was worth any wait.

What began in Japan as a dream to create cars that put out the fewest possible **pollutants** into the air has become a worldwide phenomenon. The Prius hybrid motor runs on both battery and gas power, therefore using less fuel than regular cars. As a result, it costs drivers less at the gas pump and it is better for the environment.

The Prius has improved a lot since the first model in 1997. Toyota has fixed **acceleration** problems, increased the battery power and reliability, and made the **exterior** design cooler. Now the Prius drives

The engine of a 2004 Prius was on display at a news conference to show off the ecofriendly hybrid technology.

In 2003, Harrison Ford arrived at the Academy Awards in a Prius. Many celebrities showed their support for green cars by riding in the Priuses that were rented for the event.

much like any other car without producing as many environmentally harmful pollutants. Toyota has even created an electric plug-in Prius **prototype** that it hopes to sell in 2010!

Prius drivers have benefited from more than just smaller gas bills. The U.S. government gives a tax deduction to those who purchase the car. There's a cool factor, too, especially since many celebrities have become fans of Toyota's hybrid. Actors Leonardo DiCaprio and Cameron Diaz drive the Prius. DiCaprio once owned four Priuses. For the 2003 Academy Awards, Toyota provided five Priuses to **chauffeur** stars to the red carpet. Since then, big Hollywood stars, including Jennifer Aniston, Will Ferrell, Jack Nicholson, and Brad Pitt, have bought the cars.

Of course, there has been some resistance. Some drivers are concerned that the Prius cannot accelerate as quickly as **conventional** cars, though technological advances are getting it closer. Others complain about the price: The car costs a few thousand dollars more than many American sedans. There have been reports of mechanical failures, which stopped some drivers from buying the Prius. But for those who care about the environment and want to do something to slow global warming, the Prius is a great solution.

Since its **debut**, the Prius has inspired many copycats. The car's success suggests hybrids may be the future of automobiles.

Toyota showed off its Prius plug-in hybrid electric vehicle prototype at the 2008 North American Auto Show. The prototype runs on two battery packs.

CHAPTER TWO

PLUGGING INTO NEW IDEAS

Back in 1993, when Bill Clinton was president, the United States decided to look into building automobiles that used less gas. The goal was to get 80 miles per gallon (34 kilometers per liter), and the project was supposed to take ten years. Every American automaker was invited to join in. When Toyota, a Japanese automaker, asked to be involved, the response was clear: U.S. companies only.

Talk about a bad move.

The decision to exclude Toyota, Honda, and other foreign car manufacturers wasn't too popular. In fact, when Toyota received the news, it decided to fight back. So, in January 1994, ten Toyota **executives** met to discuss the future of cars. Their goal was to create a car that used less energy and was friendlier to the environment.

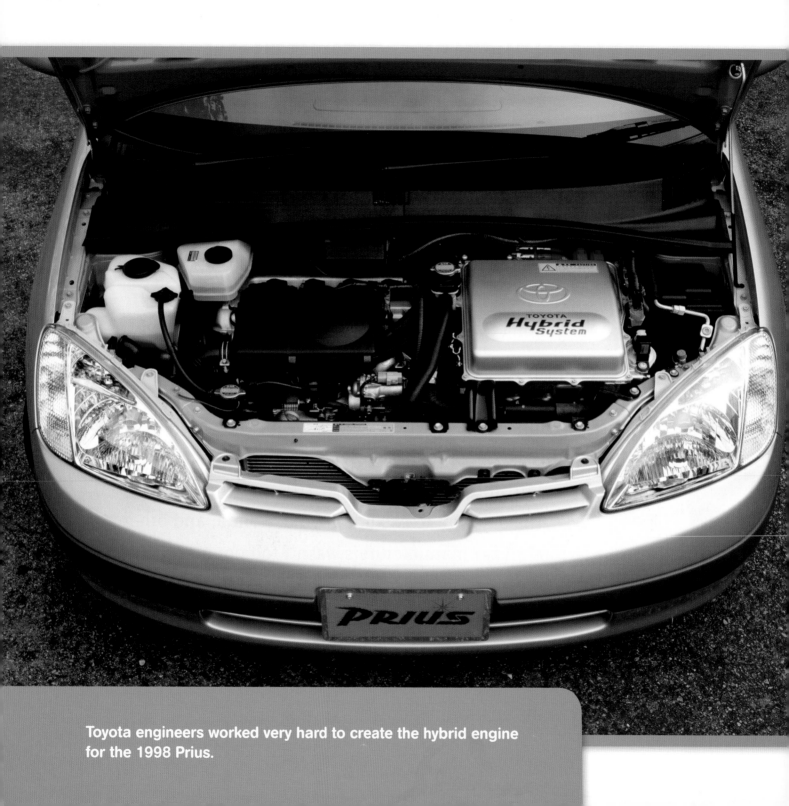

Toyota engineers worked very hard to create the hybrid engine for the 1998 Prius.

This was new territory for Toyota. For years it had based its success on copying and improving other companies' ideas. This time, Toyota wanted to be out front. It wanted to be the first company to manufacture a hybrid car for the general public.

Toyota planned to build a car that used a combination of gas and battery power. This vehicle would be more energy **efficient**, because it used less gas, and better for the environment, because the battery would not produce the clouds of poisonous smoke that came from a fuel-powered engine. Toyota started building prototypes in 1995, hoping to debut the vehicle in 1998. There were problems, of course. Some of the models wouldn't start. Others could go only a few hundred yards before shutting down. Toyota created eighty different models before narrowing the field to four. The company was making progress.

But it wasn't going fast enough for new president Hiroshi Okuda. He wanted to put the Prius—Latin for "to go before"—on the market in 1997, a year earlier than initially planned. Instead of having three years to finish the job, the design team now had two. The pressure was on.

Toyota engineers continued to have problems, however. The battery pack couldn't provide enough power to make the car go fast and it struggled in hot or cold temperatures. Though there were 1,000 engineers working on the project, they couldn't find a solution.

Hiroshi Okuda, president of Toyota, unveiled the Prius in Japan in 1997.

In March 1997 Okuda announced that the Prius would be introduced by December. When the engineers let some members of the media drive the car that May at the Tokyo Motor Show, they limited the ride to just two laps around a test track. The battery couldn't take any more.

Time was running out, but Toyota engineers were making progress. The Prius debuted in October 1997, two months ahead of Okuda's schedule and fourteen months ahead of the company's original schedule. By December the car, which squeezed 66 miles from a gallon (28 km/l) of gas—twice as much as Toyota's next most fuel-efficient car—was in showrooms and available for purchase in Japan. Despite the odds, the Prius had arrived.

But it still had a long way to go.

Though Toyota did not redesign the Prius for 2009, the car is a top-seller in the U.S. market.

CHAPTER THREE
HYBRID HYPE

Toyota's Prius team had to work long, hard hours to stick to the tight schedule. It created something truly unique and established the company as a leader in the **ecofriendly** car market. However, hopes were not high for the car. While the 1997 Toyota Camry sold a monthly average of 33,083 models, Toyota only expected to sell 1,000 Priuses a month.

Boy, were they wrong. The demand was double the original **projection**. The Prius, while not a raging success, had certainly found an enthusiastic group of buyers in Japan. The next step, however, would be tougher: Toyota had to convince Americans to buy the Prius.

An interested buyer in San Francisco, California, takes a Prius for a test drive in 2005. Rising gas prices and increased awareness about global warming have made many people consider buying a hybrid vehicle.

This time, Toyota decided not to hurry into things. The company hoped to start delivering the Prius to American drivers in late 2000. Toyota executives first wanted to make sure the car was well-received in Japan and fix any design or engine **flaws** that might prevent American drivers from purchasing the vehicle.

Toyota dealers in the United States thought the Prius was okay, but not great. Larry Miller, the owner of nine dealerships, liked the way the Prius drove, but thought the design needed work. Like Miller, many dealers were not impressed by the look of the Prius. Others were worried about the car's ability to reach top speeds. The price was also fairly high for a compact car. Perhaps the biggest **obstacle**, however, was that the Prius was extremely different from the cars that Americans usually bought.

Toyota wasn't afraid to bring the Prius to the United States. The company displayed the Prius at auto shows, created opportunities for interested buyers to exchange information online, and worked hard to make sure the car would be up to American standards. Finally, in July 2000, Toyota started to sell the Prius in the United States.

Americans loved it. Instead of putting the car in showrooms and letting people come in off the street to buy it, Toyota took orders

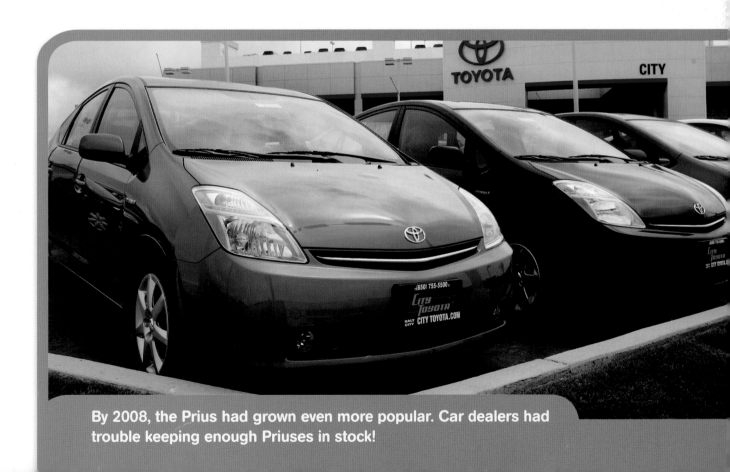

By 2008, the Prius had grown even more popular. Car dealers had trouble keeping enough Priuses in stock!

A Toyota factory worker installs a hybrid-system battery in a 2004 Prius. Employees had to work hard to keep up with the demand for the new model.

online and delivered cars to drivers as they were built. This created a huge delay, since there wasn't a ready-to-drive supply, but it also made Prius a must-have.

In 2000, Toyota sold 5,562 Prius models in only five months. The number ballooned to 15,556 models in 2001. Meanwhile, the awards were piling up. *Ward's AutoWorld* magazine named the Prius hybrid engine one of the "10 Best Engines of 2001." The Society of Automotive Engineering International called the Prius the "Best Engineered Car of 2001." Sales continued to increase in 2002 as Americans bought a whopping 20,119 models.

The hybrid car had officially arrived on the automotive scene. It was popular among people who wanted a more environmentally friendly vehicle, who wanted to save money on fuel, or who wanted to drive the latest innovation in cars. Although other automakers tried to compete by introducing hybrid models of their own, Toyota had a huge head start.

And things were only going to get better. While the first-generation Prius was gaining popularity in America and throughout the world, Toyota was working on the next version, which was set to debut in 2003. With the new model, Toyota wanted to focus on the car's look, power, and technology. They wanted the Prius to have more selling points than just a hybrid engine so that sales would continue to be strong once other hybrid models became available.

CHAPTER FOUR
THE CAR OF THE FUTURE

*T*he critics were out there. That much was true. The Prius had sold itself to the world as an ecofriendly car that reduced air pollution, making it less harmful to people, plants, and animals than gas-fueled vehicles.

But some folks complained that its added cost—the Prius was about $3,000 more expensive than similar, gas-powered cars—was more money than the amount most drivers would save in gas prices. Others even questioned Toyota's reason for building the Prius, saying it was less about helping the environment and more about helping the company's profits.

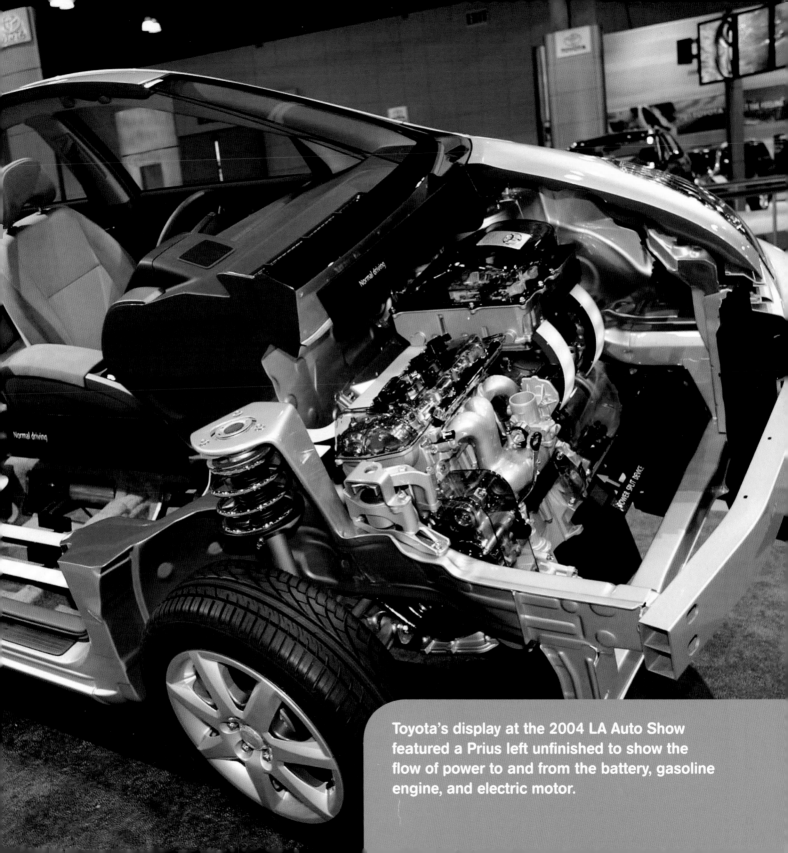

Toyota's display at the 2004 LA Auto Show featured a Prius left unfinished to show the flow of power to and from the battery, gasoline engine, and electric motor.

Don Esmond, senior vice president of Toyota, poses with a Prius and the 2004 North American Car of the Year Award. The Prius was the first hybrid to win the award.

Jim Press, president of Toyota's U.S. division, insisted that the Prius wasn't about money. "Does it save enough money to pay for itself?" he asked. "That's not the idea. What's the true cost of a gallon of gas?" He meant that this wasn't about the three or four dollars people were paying at the pump. This was about how reducing the amount of gas used worldwide could benefit the environment.

The Prius continued to sell as hybrid cars became more popular. In 2004 the vice chairman of General Motors, America's biggest automaker, admitted that his company had made a mistake by not exploring hybrid possibilities.

The second-generation Prius was introduced at the 2003 New York Auto Show. It had more power, better mileage, and produced fewer poisonous **emissions** than the original model. Toyota had improved its look, made the Prius more reliable, and created more room for passengers. The new version of the Prius could easily go 100 miles per hour (161 km/h). The Prius had grown up and was ready for a more competitive market. *Motor Trend* named it the 2004 Car of the Year. *Car & Driver* magazine said it was one of the ten best cars of 2004.

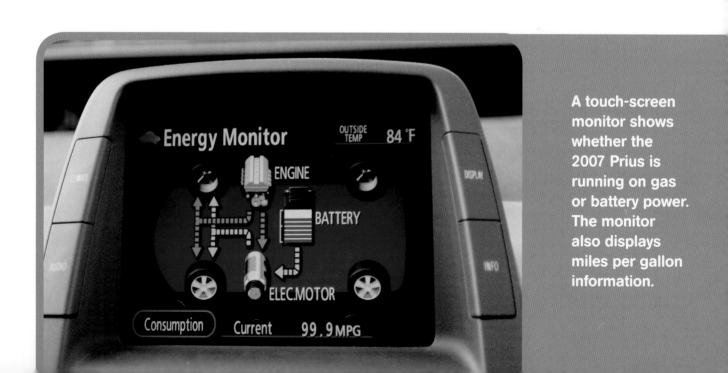

A touch-screen monitor shows whether the 2007 Prius is running on gas or battery power. The monitor also displays miles per gallon information.

American buyers were as enthusiastic as the car magazines and signed up to buy the Prius. Some insurance companies gave discounts to Prius drivers. People were willing to wait four months for a car that got 50 to 60 miles per gallon (21 to 25.5 km/l). More importantly, it was worth it for the environment. The sales figures proved Toyota had made the right move. By the end of 2004, nearly 50,000 models were being sold in America each year. By 2008 there were more than one million Prius drivers worldwide.

Toyota announced in 2008 that the next Prius would be bigger and better. Although some complained that a hybrid's job was not to compete with mainstream models, Toyota knew it needed to make the Prius roomier and give it some more power on the highway. However,

The 2009 Prius has more passenger space than earlier models, making it a great choice for families that want an ecofriendly vehicle.

The new plug-in Prius gets even better mileage than the regular hybrid model.

Toyota wanted to be even more ecofriendly and wanted to reduce the car's **carbon monoxide** output.

As part of its efforts to make the Prius even more energy efficient, Toyota created a prototype plug-in hybrid electric vehicle (PHEV). The vehicle uses two Prius battery packs that recharge when plugged into a regular outlet just like the ones for TVs and microwaves.

Toyota executives decided to start manufacturing the Prius in Mississippi. State residents were thrilled by the news and the company hoped that, by producing the car in the United States, they would further increase the Prius's popularity among Americans.

By being the first hybrid car to make a splash in the mass market, Toyota's Prius forced other automakers to look at how their cars impacted the environment. It also caused many drivers to look at the mileage and emissions of their vehicles.

The Prius is still leading the hybrid pack.

Vital Statistics

1998 Prius

Engine Size: 91.5 ci / 1.5L
Engine Type: DOHC 4-cylinder
Electric Motor Power: 288 V
Battery Type: Nickel-Metal Hydride
Battery Power: 288 V
Weight: 1,240 lbs (562 kg)
Top Speed: 98 mph (158 km/h)
0–60 mph (0–96.5 km/h): 14.1 sec

SPECIAL FACT:
Gets an estimated 48 miles per gallon (20.5 km/l)!

2009 Prius

Engine Size: 91.5 ci / 1.5L
Engine Type: DOHC 4-cylinder
Electric Motor Power: 500 V
Battery Type: Nickel-Metal Hydride
Battery Power: 201.6 V
Weight: 2,932 lbs (1,330 kg)
Top Speed: 110 mph (177 km/h)
0–60 mph (0–96.5km/h): 10.1 sec

GLOSSARY

acceleration	A car's ability to speed up.
alternative fuel	A material for fuel that does not come from fossil fuels (including petroleum).
carbon monoxide	A poisonous gas produced by automobiles that makes air less breathable and can be harmful to plants.
chauffeur	To drive a passenger to a destination.
conserve	To avoid wasteful use of something.
conventional	Ordinary and accepted.
debut	The first time something appears in public.
ecofriendly	Causes little harm to the environment.
efficient	Productive without wasting time, effort, or money.
emissions	Materials, such as smoke, put out into the air by a car or machine.
executives	The people in charge of a business.
exterior	The outside; the part of something that is seen.
flaws	Defects or errors.
global warming	An increase in the temperature of Earth's air and oceans because the Sun's heat is trapped by a layer of gases from pollution.
hybrid	A combination of two or more things. A hybrid car runs on a combination of gas and electricity.
obstacle	Something that stands in the way of successfully completing a job.

pollutants	Materials, usually man-made, that make the air, ground, or water dirty or impure. This contamination of the environment is called pollution.
projection	A guess of future sales based on current information.
prototype	The first model developed that is the pattern for all others.
roadster	A two-seater car with a powerful engine.
sport-utility vehicles	SUVs; lightweight trucks that can tow and carry cargo and also hold up to eight passengers.

FURTHER INFORMATION

BOOKS

Hammond, Richard. *Car Science*. New York: DK Publishing, 2008.

Welsbacher, Anne. *Earth-Friendly Design*. New York: Lerner, 2008.

WEBSITES

www.toyota.com/prius-hybrid

www.hybridcars.com

www.priusownersgroup.com

www.greencar.com

INDEX

Page numbers in **boldface** are photographs.

About the Author

MICHAEL BRADLEY is a writer and broadcaster who lives near Philadelphia. He has written for *Sports Illustrated for Kids*, *Hoop*, *Inside Stuff*, and *Slam* magazines and is a regular contributor to Comcast SportsNet in Philadelphia.